Finding Grace
in the 21st Century Wilderness

Brenda M. Stokes

©Copyright 2022 Brenda Stokes

All rights reserved. This book is protected under the copyright laws of the United States of America.

ISBN: 978-1-954609-41-9

No portion of this book may be reproduced, distributed, or transmitted in any form, including photocopying, recording, or other electronic or mechanical methods, without the written permission of the publisher, except in the case of brief quotations embodied in reviews and certain other non-commercial uses permitted by copyright law. Permission granted on request.

For information regarding special discounts for bulk purchases, please contact LaBoo Publishing Enterprise at staff@laboopublishing.com.

Scripture taken from the New King James Version®. Copyright © 1982 by Thomas Nelson. Used by permission. All rights reserved.

The Holy Bible, King James Version. Cambridge Edition: 1769; King James Bible Online, 2019. www.kingjamesbibleonline.org.

Scripture quotations marked TPT are from The Passion Translation®. Copyright © 2017, 2018 by Passion & Fire Ministries, Inc. Used by permission. All rights reserved. ThePassionTranslation.com.

Scripture quotations marked (NLT) are taken from the Holy Bible, New Living Translation, copyright ©1996, 2004, 2015 by Tyndale House Foundation. Used by permission of Tyndale House Publishers, Inc., Carol Stream, Illinois 60188. All rights reserved

Table of Contents

Preface xix

Introduction 1

Chapter 1: Grace in the Wilderness 3

Chapter 2: If Only. 9

Chapter 3: Who Is on the Lord's Side?. 15

Chapter 4: Where Grace Found Me. 23

Chapter 5: The Inheritance Factor 27

References 35

About the Author 37

Endorsements

God has a way of placing among us those unique individuals who possess within them burdens for the lost. Brenda's concern and love for mankind are detailed in this book. She will show us where we were, where we are and where we are headed. Through the book you will feel her passion for the lost and hear her cry for the church to rid itself of spiritual deficiencies that inhibit our ability to experience the grace, the undeserved, unmerited, unearned, kindness and favor of God (Robert Morris). I am so very proud that she has put her passion to paper, revealing the heart we should have for the lost.

Your Loving Husband
Lewis L. Stokes, Sr.
Vice Presiding Bishop, United Church of Jesus Christ (Apostolic)

Anyone desiring encouragement and a spiritual lift must read this book, Finding Grace In The 21st Century Wilderness does that for me. As a pastor, I am always in need of material to use to bless people under my care, of which this is one. In addition, as a result of assorted life-threatening illnesses, when "going through," Finding Grace is one of those reads I, or anyone, can pull off the shelf and get a boost. Then too, as one always in the hunt for illustrative material for teaching and preaching, examples from Brenda Stokes and the scriptures fits that need.

Further, Brenda says practical things that resonate with me. When struggling with the vicissitudes of life, we sometimes lose perspective, preferring the comfort zone of "what was" then blame God in saying, "If only God had, or if only He would . . ." Then, Finding Grace snaps us back to the reality that, not only are we to trust in God's faithfulness to see us through, but understand that others in need of grace are observing our character in the process. Others are impacted by our character responses "in the wilderness."

Finally, I am a little more sensitive by Brenda reminding me that in this 21st Century Wilderness in which we all live, in God's mysterious way, He is molding our character for the better and for His glory.

Brenda has more than written another book. She is blessed to have lived victoriously what she writes about. Get this book, and thank Sister Stokes for yielding to the Spirit to bless us.

Bishop (Dr.) Cleven L. Jones, Sr. (DMin)
Author, Rapid Insights Bible Survey

∼

The world we live in today is very complex and suffers from much confusion, disillusionment and hopelessness. I meet people on a daily basis who seem to have lost their center and want an assurance that everything is going to be alright. What I have just described to you is called the "Wilderness" in the book entitled, *Finding Grace in the 21st Century Wilderness*. The author Elder Brenda Stokes eloquently lays out a plan to help you navigate through life's many issues by assuring us it's only been by His grace that we are not consumed by the many trials we have faced on this journey called life. I am not sure about you, but as a Pastor and an elected official, I have learned many lessons in the wilderness when I thought God was picking on me and no one was going through but me. This must-read book will help you make sense out of your wilderness experience. So when you emerge from what some would call a low place, but God calls it a learning place, I strongly believe this book will help you gain a better understanding of his Grace and his power to deliver you out of all of your troubles. It is a must read for every person who has come out of the wilderness because of a desire to be better, bolder, and blessed.

Pastor Steven L. Brown
Senior Pastor, Faith Temple Ministries (Apostolic)
Suffolk, VA

∽

It gives me great pleasure to endorse Finding Grace In The 21st Century Wilderness. It is a dynamic read for all of us that are on the backside of COVID-19, because saints are still going through, and some feel nobody cares or understands, but thanks be to God for this book. It's a word of great encouragement for those of us in the role of Leadership. May God speak to you in the pages of this little read.

Bishop Michael D. Bull
Senior Pastor, Saint Matthew United Church of Jesus Christ
Darlington, SC

∽

In an age where many are perplexed and polarized in the midst of the current political climate and pandemic aftermath, Pastor Brenda Stokes offers a voice of reason to those who may be both wondering and wandering in this 21st century wilderness era. She masterfully takes us on a journey with her to reveal answers from a biblical perspective to address the conundrum of questions that many have posed to discover how we can find God's grace even in the most bewildering times that humankind faces. This book serves as a clarion call to those who desire to serve God without compromising their faith or morality. We commend this book to you and recommend it as a resource of hope to be shared with others.

Bishop L. W. III and Dr. Natalie A. Francisco
Oversight Pastors, C3 Hampton and Calvary Covenant Ministries, Inc.

∽

Finding Grace in the 21st Century Wilderness is a fresh reminder that God's abundant grace is available to us in wilderness places. In the face of societal crisis and cultural deterioration, God's grace stands ready as an active force that sustains and propels. Brenda M. Stokes provides a powerful message of healing, hope, and reassurance of God's presence in times of uncertainty. In a changing world, God gives us unchanging grace. This book soothes the soul, comforts the heart, and brings peace to the mind. Even in the wilderness, God's grace is unrelenting.

Dr. Tarron D. Howe,
Senior Pastor, United Family Worship Center
Hampton, VA

Lady Brenda Stokes has done an awesome, impactful presentation of comparing the wilderness experience of the children of Israel under the leadership of Moses to what we as a people are experiencing today. She has shown in a very enlightening way that there is really nothing new under the sun. I recommend all to read this work and take a self-examination of where you are in the Wilderness and see where the Lord is leading you on this journey of the 21st Century. I do believe after reading this that it will not take forty years for you to accept the direction that God has for your life.

Dr. Robert E. Johnson, Sr.-Bishop
New Jerusalem Praise Tabernacle
Baltimore, MD

Brenda Stokes has given us an insightful, readable interpretation of life today against the backdrop of life among the people of God in Biblical times. I especially enjoyed her use of Scripture, anecdotes and personal testimony throughout her writing. I enthusiastically recommend it!

Bishop Lewis M. Payne
Senior Pastor, Word for the World Community Church
Stewartstown, PA

It dawned on me at first glance reading the title: *Finding Grace in the 21st Century Wilderness*, that many of us made it into the 21st century but very few of us will make it out alive. It is important to know that throughout the centuries, God's grace has always been extended to us in the wilderness. Through her personal experiences, it is a real blessing that Elder Brenda Stokes has taken the time to provide us with a (GPS) Grace Positioning System that will allow us to navigate this journey through our current wilderness journey. Thank You

Bishop Don diXon Williams
Executive Board
United Church of Jesus Christ (Apostolic)

Dedication

In Memory of
Timothy and Arlena Dawson Parks
&
To
Eliza Smith Jones
Who Laid My Spiritual Foundation
To
My Beloved Husband
and
Mentor Extraordinaire
Bishop Lewis L. Stokes, Sr.

Foreword

Freedom and prosperities have become idols we substitute for an authentic relationship with God. A sense of spiritual independence leads us away from the only one who can help us through the present malaise of our times. It is indeed a wilderness experience through which special grace is needed to navigate.

Finding Grace in the 21st Century Wilderness is an honest reflection by one who has experienced and observed people who claim Christian identity but who live based on human effort. At the core of this is an inability to trust God and his plan for their lives. God's grace informs and empowers one to do and respond to the many and inevitable disruptions of life. Finding Grace... exposes an arrogance of impatience and disobedience which leads to pre-empting the grace available to us.

The Apostle Paul writing to the church at Philippi encourages them to "...obey God with deep reverence and fear.

For God is working in you, giving you the desire and the power to do what pleases him." (Philippians 2:12b-13, NLT). This is the grace that is available to give us the knowledge of his will and the grace to do it.

Elder Stokes connects her personal experience to scriptural lessons that undergird the message of the **Grace of God** that is available to any who would obey him and trust him through their life journey in this 21st Century Wilderness.

+Monroe Saunders, Jr., D.Min. Presiding Bishop, United Church of Jesus Christ (Apostolic)

Acknowledgments

It seems a slight to overlook anyone who played a part in my spiritual journey, but for those who encouraged me in this particular work, I want to say a very special, "THANK YOU!" First and foremost, thank you to two individuals who kept encouraging me to put pen to paper. First is my beloved husband Bishop Lewis L. Stokes, who assured me that I could do this, and secondly is Bishop Cleven Jones, who reminded me that "timing is everything" when writing a book. To our Presiding Bishop, Bishop Monroe Saunders, Jr., thank you so much for taking time from your busy schedule to write the Foreword. For everyone who prayed, wrote words of endorsement or testimonials in support of this, my first book, please know that I am eternally grateful.

Brenda M. Stokes

Preface

I've always loved writing. I was raised by an educator and have had many opportunities to put pen to paper. However, being called to scribe something that would cause us, the people of God, to pause and reflect on our behavior was something entirely different and admittedly, quite challenging.

As Co-Pastor of a church for 16 years, I've witnessed the good and not so good. I've seen everything from sold-out commitment to situations where God was a priority only until He was no longer needed and where, once the problem was solved, everything became more important than God and His instruction. Then came COVID-19 where we all, saved and unsaved, were on equal footing. Sadly, those of us who claimed Jesus as Lord began to point the finger at the unsaved. Surely this was about their behavior when, truth be told, it was God calling His church to Marah. *Finding Grace in the 21st Century Wilderness* was written to help us understand and value the wilderness experience in which we presently find ourselves, and prayerfully benefit from its many difficult lessons.

Brenda M Stokes

Introduction

Like many, during the past few years, I've cried out to the Lord for forgiveness for the sinful ways of this country. I asked Him to extend His grace to those of us who, though not perfect, are committed to righteous living. I've asked him to withhold his wrath. I've asked him to give us all another chance.

I have been sort of like Nehemiah when he received news of how bad things were in Jerusalem after it was besieged. He wept first, and then he repented. He took responsibility for his role and that of his brethren for the condition they found themselves in (Nehemiah 1:1-7).

There is no getting around the fact that where we are as a nation today is due, in large part, to the fact that we have made the freedoms and prosperities that God has so graciously afforded us <u>our new god</u>!

How do you know? Well, when we get overwhelmed in this thing called life, what is the first thing we walk away from? When we don't get the answer we want, who and what do we put on trial for all that we are going through? Certainly not our precious way of life.

So, I asked myself: how do we find grace in this 21st century wilderness? Before we can do this, we must understand what grace is, and what a wilderness entails.

CHAPTER 1:
Grace in the Wilderness

And He said to me, "My grace is sufficient for you, for My strength is made perfect in weakness"
—2 Corinthians 12:9a (NKJV)

One of my favorite functional definitions of grace is "God choosing to bless us rather than curse us as our sin deserves. It is His benevolence to the undeserving." [1]

As I pondered that, it came to me that while mercy withholds a punishment we deserve, grace offers us a better way. In prayer, the Lord revealed to me that it is indeed "sustenance." Sustenance, or a sustaining portion, is the amount that is needed. Only God knows what we need (of anything) and how much we can handle. His grace is measured. In 2 Corinthians 12:9 the Lord reminds the

Apostle Paul that it is sufficient, even in our weakness. It sustains us, nourishes us. It replenishes us in our darkest hour and it is extended to bring us closer to God. Grace is that power of God that exceeds what we could achieve or hope for by our own labors.

Our grandmothers used to say, about any Godsend: "It wasn't nothing but the grace of God." Well, to experience this grace, we must not only have a relationship with God, but be in communion with Him. We must acknowledge Him as our watchful master. We have to want Him in our business. We can't be scurrying around as we are now, trying to figure things out on our own, especially those of us who claim to have made Him "Lord" of our lives.

We are told in Exodus 32 that Moses goes up on the mountain to seek the Lord on Israel's behalf and he stays longer than they think he should, so they are tempted by the devil to come up with a god of their own. When Moses came down from Mount Sinai with the tables written by God and found that the people had made themselves a god (a golden calf) and were worshiping him, he became so angry that he broke the tables and confronted Aaron as to how he could allow such a thing. Aaron responded, and I'll use today's vernacular, "Well, that's what they wanted, and nobody knew where you were. So, I just took the gold and cast it in the fire and this calf came out." While we know his explanation wasn't entirely true, we must ask ourselves, "What are we casting into the fire and producing in the 21st century: greed, fame, fortune, tolerance, racism, bigotry, thievery, dishonesty? What wilderness have we created?"

A wilderness by common definition is "those last truly wild places that humans do not control and have not developed with roads, pipelines or other industrial infrastructure" (Wikipedia). However, we've discovered the wilderness of the bible is a "liminal space—an in-between place where ordinary life is suspended, identity shifts, and new possibilities emerge" [2] (Jenny Phillips, *Jesus and Wilderness*). Through the experiences of the Israelites in exile, we learn that while the biblical wilderness is a place of danger, temptation and chaos, it is also a place for solitude, nourishment, and revelation from God (American Bible Society). Some years back, during the government shutdown, the Lord stirred in my spirit that we (as a nation) were in a wilderness. Like the children of Israel, we didn't like it, we couldn't control it, and honestly, we'd rather have been sustained by that which kept us in bondage. It was impossible for many of us to see its constructive purpose.

Dennis Reynolds stated that "bible stories about people in the 'wilderness' almost always show that they were there for a particular time, and for a constructive purpose. They had to manage with what they had until they discovered that they were in a place of spiritual resource. Then, they not only utilized what they already had, but received more, from the resource."

"Please can somebody tell me how long we will be in this 21st century wilderness and what purpose it serves?" Those are the questions we have heard increasingly over the past few years, and in some cases, even those that took us there couldn't decide how long it should last nor come up with a constructive purpose. Well, when God sends His people into a wilderness situation, He knows for how long and for what purpose. We are where we are not only for a season, but for a reason.

When the children of Israel crossed the Red Sea, they came upon the waters of Marah which were too bitter to drink, so they complained to Moses. Moses sought God about the matter and the Lord showed him a piece of wood that he threw into the water, making it good to drink.

The purpose of the Marah experience was two-fold: it was an opportunity to set a standard of obedience to God and to (once again) prove His sufficiency.[26] He said, "if you will listen carefully to the voice of the Lord your God and do what is right in his sight, obeying his commands and keeping all his decrees, then I will not make you suffer any of the diseases I sent on the Egyptians; for I am the lord who heals you"

[27] After leaving Marah, the Israelites traveled on to the Oasis of Elim, where they found twelve springs and seventy palm trees. They camped there beside the water. (Exodus 15:26-27)

He has their attention, at least for now. But how many know that an Omniscient God was fully aware that they needed much more work, just as we in the 21st century do?

By their complaining, it took Israel 40 years to make an 11-day journey and the challenges of the wilderness convinced them that despite all God had done for them, He was not truly going to bring them into a land flowing with milk and honey. Is that what has happened to Christians in America? Have we decided that what we have in this country is as good as it gets, and thus begun to turn away from God, thinking that perhaps He has no intention of us ruling with Him?

CHAPTER 2:
If Only

Is this not the word that we told you in Egypt, saying,
"Let us alone that we may serve the Egyptians"?
For it would have been better for us to serve the
Egyptians than that we should die in the wilderness.
—Exodus 14:12 (NKJV)

Given enough stress, even people of God have a tendency to reflect on "what was". Despite the pain things of the past may have brought, when compared to the wilderness, "what was" is sometimes preferred. Unfortunately though, in the wilderness, it is easy to blame God: "If only God had or if only He would…" We look at God as though He were man and unable to fix our situation. He could put a stop to it anytime He wants, but like Israel, we are in Marah, and I like the way George Warnock put it: "He leads us to Marah so we can discover the inherent bitterness of our fallen nature and shows us how to deal with it."[3] He forces us back to our Maker. Israel faced 40 years in the wilderness and the past few years in America have felt like 40 years. Every day is something different, some "Breaking News." But only God knows what it takes to get our attention…to change us…to reconcile us to Himself. For them it was 40 years. For us, I don't know.

Israel had an "If Only" moment.

Exodus 16: ² There, too, the whole community of Israel complained about Moses and Aaron.³ "If only the Lord had killed us back in Egypt," they moaned. "There we sat around pots filled with meat and ate all the bread we wanted. But now you have brought us into this wilderness to starve us all to death."

Murmuring and complaining, they asked (and I'm paraphrasing), "What do we do now God? YOU brought us here, so what do we do now?" You see, in a wilderness, we put God and His representatives on trial. We blame Him for us going back into sin. God says we spend years in sin, and when He delivers us, the first thing we do is put Him on trial. If He doesn't cause an immediate change to our situation, we say, "I'll just go back to doing what I know works." Lest we think this was limited to the culture of 13th century BC, I recently read an article by Dr. Carol Peters-Tanksley entitled "The Most Overlooked Obstacle to Maturity and Wholeness." In it, she states that "our contemporary culture has fueled our natural human tendency toward instant gratification." [4] In other words, we want it, and we want it NOW! Nowhere have we witnessed this more than during COVID-19. We literally hounded the medical community for tests and a vaccine, and we put our own timetable on a PANDEMIC. When we had had enough, WE decided it was over, even with people still dying. We rejected the science as a hoax, and many subsequently rejected God. But as I've learned, God doesn't put us in a wilderness situation to leave us, but to see if we will leave Him. He puts us there to bring us closer to him. That is precisely what our country is faced with now: a call to return to God.

Much like the children of Israel when they were in Egypt, we as a nation have been sustained by that which holds us captive: Medicaid, Food Stamps, Government Subsidized Housing, Disability, Stimulus Checks, Unemployment, PPP Loans, and the list goes on. While there is nothing wrong with getting help, we have become imprisoned by those who tell us if we can qualify, when we can qualify and how much we can qualify for—even for benefits we've earned. But God says, "I have better for you, but I can't give it to you until I get your attention. Sometimes I have to make things uncomfortable to get you to OBEY me. I have to do things that even confound those around you. They think they are in control (the pharaohs, the presidents, the congress and the courts), but I have allowed it, to bring you close to me. I want you to learn to depend on me, and just like I never forsook them in days of old, I'll never forsake you. If I am able to bring you into a land flowing with milk and honey, surely, I am able to sustain you till you get there."

There are those watching us very closely right now to see if we buckle under pressure, to see if our character is befitting the Christians we claim to be or whether we will build idols to worship and turn back. Hebrews 10:39 (KJV) says, "But we are not of them who draw back unto perdition; but of them that believe to the saving of the soul." So, we must ask ourselves: Will we exhibit the character, faith and obedience of a Christian in the midst of all we are going through, will we allow it to bring us closer in our walk with the Lord, or will we hope for it to be over, only to return to the things God is trying to rid us of?

You see, we've had a number of these wilderness situations of late: hurricanes, tornados, sequestration, government shutdown, racial profiling and police brutality, bold re-emergence of white supremacy, gay rights, mass murders in schools, churches, night clubs and grocery stores, Covid-19, election lies, drug culture, child endangerment, storming of the capital, the war in Ukraine, and the list goes on. Ordinary life suspended, identity shifted, but new possibilities emerged. How so?

Wilderness situations tended to level the playing field—no matter how rich or how poor you were. You didn't have lights, nor did others. You stood in lines, paid high prices for gas, just like others. You spoke to people you wouldn't ordinarily speak to and so did others. You sought a God that you may have been separated from for quite some time. So did others. You even shared what you had with those who had less. You protested, wrote letters to your congressmen, wore masks, took rounds of vaccinations and may have even voted for the first time in your life. So did many others. The wilderness causes us to do this. But like the children of Israel, it causes some other things too.

Pastor George Belobaba said, "The wilderness determines whether God or the flesh is going to rule your life." Will I or will I not hear and OBEY the voice of the Lord?[5]

Deuteronomy 8:2-3 (KJV) teaches "...and thou shalt remember all the way which the Lord thy god led thee these forty years in the wilderness, to humble thee, and to prove thee, to know what was in thine heart, whether thou wouldest keep his commandments, or no. And he humbled thee, and suffered thee to hunger, and fed thee with manna, which thou knewest not, neither did thy fathers know; that He might make thee know that man doth not live by bread only, but by every word that proceedeth out of the mouth of the Lord doth man live." It was God who led them there, and it is God who led us here. But it was also God who kept them through it and is keeping us. So, we must ask ourselves: "Would I rather go back (to what was) than accept the molding and calibrating that will assure me of a life with God?" All we have to compare it to, is where we've been.

CHAPTER 3:
Who Is on the Lord's Side?

Now when Moses saw that the people were unrestrained (for Aaron had not restrained them, to their shame among their enemies), then Moses stood in the entrance of the camp, and said, "Whoever is on the Lord's side—come to me!"—Exodus 32:25-26a (NKJV)

In Exodus 32:26 (KJV) we are told that Moses, frustrated with the murmurings of Israel, stands in the gate of the camp and says: "Who is on the Lord's side? Let him come unto me." Saints, we are at such a place of reckoning in this country. We are at a place where, if we want the grace of God extended to us, we must make a choice in how we will live out our lives and trust God to help us to do it. I don't want you to get the notion that we can do anything to earn the favor of God, but rather that we must be in such a relationship, close enough to Him, that we can be assured that He's watching over us. In Luke 15:11-32 we find the story of The Prodigal Son, where the Father represents God. Bishop Lewis L. Stokes recently shared, "It was only when the Prodigal returned home and his father received him and reconciled him to a place of sonship, that the Prodigal fully understood the grace of God." Again, we have to want Him in our business.

Let's look again at Israel. Moses pleads with God not to destroy Israel, but God says, "Whoever has sinned against me I will blot out of my book." So, He punishes Israel greatly. But worse, He withdraws Himself from them—calling them "stiff-necked." Nothing could be worse than to have God withdraw Himself from you. Has this modern society become stiff-necked, "calling unclean clean and unholy holy"? Moses again meets with God and he pleads with Him, saying, "You're telling me to go ahead, to take Your people to the promised land, but if we don't have Your Presence abiding with us, don't take us up from here, for we will surely fail." "For how then will it be known that Your people and I have found grace in your sight, except You go with us?" (Exodus 33:16 NKJV). I dare you to look in the mirror and say, "If I don't have the grace of God abiding with me, I won't survive this wilderness."

Mahalia Jackson sang a hymn that said: "Without God, I could do nothing. Without Him, I would fail. Without

God, my life would be rugged (drifting), like a ship without a sail." [6]

We are wondering why life is so rugged and why we are going through what we're going through—why we're having so many challenges in life. Could it be we are living a life of disobedience, one without God? Could it be that we have put our trust in chariots, and horses? But we are told, "Be not deceived, God is not mocked. Whatsoever a man soweth, that shall he also reap" (Galatians 6:7 NKJV). God still knows how to bring us to Marah and remove whatever becomes a God to us besides himself.

About three years ago, I read a Facebook post with an exhaustive list of indicators of how far our country has fallen on the humanitarian scale. It included the following just to name a few:

>Repeal and replace Obamacare

>Cancel all federal funding to "Sanctuary Cities"

>Immediately terminate Obama's "two illegal" Executive Orders i.e. DACA (which gives temporary status to those brought illegally into the country as children) and DAPA (which allows undocumented parents of US citizens to remain in country)

> Build Border Wall and eventually have Mexico pay for it
>
> Hire 5,000 Border Patrol Agents
>
> Triple the number of ICE Agents
>
> Suspend Syrian Refugee Program

It was said to be a direct lift from the "playbook" of a senior advisor in the Trump Administration, written on a White House white board. It was underscored by the originator as "a real and active threat" to him, his way of life, and all the people he loved. Some readers described it as a "Wall of Hate", one that (I believe) encapsulates the gravity of this 21st century wilderness, one that desperately needs the all-sufficient and sustaining grace of God. But how do we find this grace?

First, we must accept our plight. Ralph Erskine said, "Think not that the government is out of Christ's hand when men are doing many sad things and giving many heavy blows to the work of God. No, no; men are but His hand; and it is the hand of God that justly and righteously is lying heavy upon His people." [7] Secondly, we must embrace the tenets of 2 Chronicles 7:14 – humble ourselves, pray, seek His face and turn from our wicked ways.

Humility acknowledges that "with all I know, there is more to know." It forces us into self-reflection and recognizes that "as I am, I get in the way of being a better me." Pastor Sheryl Menendez said it this way: "In order to rid ourselves of pride, we must get to the place where we hate us."

Then we are instructed to pray. Prayer is a conversation, a two-way discourse. Somebody's talking and somebody's listening. We must intentionally listen to hear what God is saying. There was a song we sang in Vacation Bible School with lyrics that truly ministered that point:

>Open my eyes, that I may see
>
>Glimpses of truth Thou hast for me;
>
>Place in my hands the wonderful key
>
>That shall unclasp and set me free.
>
>Silently now I wait for Thee,
>
>Ready my God, Thy will to see,
>
>Open my eyes, illumine me,
>
>Spirit divine!
>
>2 Open my ears that I may hear

voices of truth thou sendest clear,

and while the wave notes fall on my ear,

ev'rything false will disappear.

Silently now I wait for thee,

ready, my God, thy will to see.

Open my ears, illumine me,

Spirit divine!

Clara H. Scott, 1895 [8]

We are then challenged to seek the face of God. While there are many scriptures that speak to this, I believe Proverbs 3:5-6 (NLT) says it best:

"[5]Trust in the Lord with all your heart; do not depend on your own understanding. [6]Seek his will in all you do, and he will show you which path to take."

Lastly, we are instructed to "turn from our wicked ways." To do so, we must commit to becoming more like Christ and less like us. A good place to start is Proverbs 6:16-19 (NLT), which reads:

There are six things the Lord hates—no, seven things he detests: haughty eyes, a lying tongue, hands that kill the innocent, a heart that plots evil, feet that race to do wrong, a false witness who pours out lies, a person who sows discord in a family.

If we want to experience the grace of God, we must embrace these tenets not as a popular "pandemic-era" slogan, but as an edict issued for the restoration of fellowship with God.

Sadly, much like Israel, saints of today no longer seem interested in God's way of dealing with much of anything. Many aren't interested in hearing what God has to say through His transforming word, and when that happens, He leads us to Marah. How can you say that? The evidence bears it out: First is the new 21st century standard of twice a month church attendance. Secondly, we look at our watches and squirm in our seats for God's messenger to hurry up and finish telling us what God has to say, and then spend an hour after church talking to members and friends, hearing what they have to say. We need more grace!

Why is it that we don't want to hear what God has to say? I believe it is spelled out in Hebrews 4:12, which reads, "for the word of God is living and powerful, and sharper than any two-edged sword, piercing even to the division of soul and spirit, and of joints and marrow, and it is a discerner of the thought and intents of the heart." The word of God exposes our true attitudes, weaknesses, our feelings and desires. It exposes our preference to depend upon ourselves and others, rather than depend on God.

I am reminded of Exodus 20, at Sinai, when the Lord spoke His commandments to Israel and the people were so terrified that they said to Moses, "[19]Speak thou with us, and we will hear: but let not God speak with us, lest we die.

"[20]And Moses said unto the people, Fear not: for God is come to PROVE you, and that his fear may be before your faces, that ye sin not. [21]And the people stood afar off, and Moses drew near unto the thick darkness where God was."

God's instruction then, is designed to PROVE us, purify us, and thus draw us near to Him, not to push us away, as our sin deserves. Hebrews 4:16 invites us to "Come boldly to the throne of grace, that we may obtain mercy and find grace to help in the time of need." Coming to Jesus must be an act of willful obedience and confidence, not one of timidity. Again, we seek Him because we want Him in our business, because we need what only His sustaining grace can provide. We seek Him knowing, as my beloved husband once preached, "His grace awaits." When we draw near to God, He draws near to us. He will not accept us in our sin, but when we abandon it, He graciously, lovingly accepts us.

CHAPTER 4:
Where Grace Found Me

*And God is able to make all grace abound toward you,
that you, always having all sufficiency in all things,
may have an abundance for every good work.*
—2 Corinthians 9:8 (NKJV)

One of the many things we've discovered about grace is that it will find us at our lowest point. I can fully attest to this. But for the grace of God, I could never have survived the period in my life between December 5, 1996–July 7, 1999. It was during these 2.5 years that my late husband succumbed to leukemia, my mother was diagnosed with Parkinson's disease, and my father, having been diagnosed with an advanced stage of lung cancer, shot himself to death in my home.

Soon afterwards, I was notified that the government contract to which I was assigned was coming to an end, with no renewal in sight. My mother, despite her physical challenges, was still a prayer warrior, and upon hearing the news of our situation, got down on her knees and prayed perhaps the most radical prayer I had ever heard. The very next day, I received a call from a friend expressing concern about my employment situation and asking if she could recommend me to her company. I agreed. That same afternoon, I received a call that led to an interview the very next day. After a wonderful lunch and an extensive interview, I was offered a project management position, with the caveat that I could not begin until the new contract was awarded, which was at least 60 days away. I reluctantly agreed to accept the position and it was then **that grace took over.** The manager said, "You know what? I really don't want to lose someone with your talent. We have several contracts in this area for which we have no real oversight. We are spread too thin. I am going to ask for permission to bring you on NOW, as a program manager, with the stipulation that you will be project manager for the new contract once it's awarded." Talk about grace finding me! As you can imagine, the salary for this "newly created" position was considerably more than the one I had interviewed for. Remember, God's grace is sufficient. He knows exactly how much we need and can handle, of anything.

In the words of a renowned Preacher: "Let's go deeper."

CHAPTER 4: WHERE GRACE FOUND ME

On Sunday morning, January 7, 2001, I entered my former church, fully prepared to sit where I always did, with a small group of sisters that I dearly loved. As I prepared to take my seat, suddenly, the Lord directed me to move. Startled, but obedient, I explained to my friends that I had to move. Not only did the Lord instruct me to move, but He moved me clear to the other side of the church. As I sat down, He said loudly this one word: "SOAK." As I heard the voice of God on that day, I knew I would never be the same. Yes, I had been in that particular ministry for over 10 years partaking of the powerful teaching and preaching and growth that it provided, but this day was different. It was the seventh day of the year, and clearly, I was leaving a place of the "rudimentary" and moving to another place in Christ. So then, why "SOAK"? My initial focus went to my leaders. I suddenly felt an urging to look more closely at them than ever before; but there was more, and I knew it had something to do with matters of maturity. But what I didn't know was…why me and why now. The secret things belong to the Lord, our God (Deuteronomy 29:29a).

The definition of SOAK as used in the King James Version is to lie in a fluid till the substance has imbibed (absorbed) what it can contain. But what does SOAKING do? I believe the answer lies in Hebrews 6:7-8 (TPT):

"*⁷For men's hearts* are just like the soil that drinks up the showers which often fall upon it. Some soil will yield crops as God's blessing upon the field. ⁸But if the field continues to produce only thorns and thistles a curse hangs over it and it will be burned."

In the natural world, soaking allows something to germinate or produce faster. In the spiritual world, soaking prepares us much the same way. It is a kind of surrender that keeps us from fighting against what God is trying to produce in and through us. It is a place of complete surrender, where we become more like Christ. "Because I have spent time with Him, this is who I have become!"

I believe that what God intended for me to see, and that He desires for all of us to see, is that we can be saved and study the word for a long time and still be too immature for where He desires to take us. There are no shortcuts in soaking or maturing. Rain is going to come, and it can be challenging. It's hard to see in the rain and it's hard to navigate in the rain; but this same SOAKING is what causes growth. What we have to decide is, "What will the soaking produce in me? Will I allow it to mature me into something that God can use, or will I allow it to produce something that will be cast into the fire and burned?"

Thankfully, my obedience met God's grace, because it was that very same year that I was connected to my beloved husband for a journey in service to Christ that continues to this very day.

CHAPTER 5:
The Inheritance Factor

And now I commend you to God and to the word of his grace, which is able to build you up and to give you the inheritance among all those who are sanctified.
—*Acts 20:32 (KJV)*

We have established that even in a wilderness, we are not exempt from temptation. But what do we do when the tempter comes? Do we hold fast to what we know is right, or do we break up with God?

Let's look at Jesus' example. Matthew 4:1 teaches that Jesus was led by the Spirit into the Desert, so that the devil could "test" him. The devil tested Him by trying to convince Him to use the power of God rather than relying on the faithfulness of God: He had fasted for forty nights, after which He was hungry, and when the tempter came to Him, he said, "If Thou be the Son of God, command that these stones be made bread." Jesus responds: "It is written, man doth not live by bread alone but by every word that proceedeth from the mouth of God." Seeing that didn't work, he leads Jesus to the highest point of the temple in Jerusalem and tells him to jump and uses scripture to coerce Him. For the scripture says, 'For He will give His angels charge over you.' Seeing that didn't work, he tries to tempt Jesus with "stuff", i.e. kingdoms. Jesus overcame His wilderness temptations by His faith in and obedience to God's word, and it propelled Him into His ministry.

The devil knows what we are hungry for and what it takes to get us to abandon our testimony. If we are hungry for affection, he knows it. If we are hungry for money, fame, or notoriety, he knows it. Most of the time, he catches us unarmed and unprepared, no prayer life, no fasting, church once in a while; and when we are unarmed, we are not sensitive to the work of the Holy Spirit, so we take counsel from other unarmed folks that lead us down the proverbial "primrose path," a path that leads to disastrous consequences.

One familiar example is found in 1 Samuel 15 where Saul disobeyed God's instruction to utterly destroy the Amalakites and all they owned, and then shifted blame (for his disobedience) to the people's desires for the spoil, which could "potentially" be used as sacrifices to God. It's like tithing from robbery money. I know it was ill-gotten, but I convince myself that if I use it for God's purpose, He will overlook it. This disobedience and self-absorbing attitude cost Saul greatly and, unfortunately, it has replicated itself among God's people. We've all heard this: "It's okay if I don't go to church as long as I'm sending my money. I'm doing what God said to do—but I'm just doing it my way," not recognizing that this choice violates the very reason given for assemblage in Hebrews 10:25, "to encourage one another."

Now that we've seen what Saul's disobedience cost him, let's look at the benefits that come with obeying God.

The scriptures depict Isaac, Abraham's child of Promise, as a hard-working, gentle man, soft spoken and one of the most incredibly humble patriarchs of the bible. Few would even take notice of somebody like Isaac—until he appeared to be "blessed." But why was he blessed? In Genesis 26:1-6 (NLT), we find the instruction he received from God and His response to it:

> 1 A severe famine now struck the land, as had happened before in Abraham's time. So Isaac moved to Gerar, where Abimelech, king of the Philistines, lived. (He was previously in Beer Lahai Roi in Canaan)
>
> 2 The Lord appeared to Isaac and said, "Do not go down to Egypt, but do as I tell you.

3 Live here as a foreigner in this land, and I will be with you and bless you. I hereby confirm that I will give all these lands to you and your descendants,[a] just as I solemnly promised Abraham, your father.

4 I will cause your descendants to become as numerous as the stars of the sky, and I will give them **all** these lands. And through your descendants all the nations of the earth will be blessed.

5 I will do this because Abraham listened to me and obeyed all my requirements, commands, decrees, and instructions."

6 So Isaac stayed in Gerar.

We see here that the release of Isaac's inheritance was not based solely on who he was born to, but it had more to do with who he had become.

KLERONEMEO is the Hebrew word for inheritance and it means: to receive by lot meaning either: (1) by birthright because of sonship, or (2) by obedience and faithfulness to God amid opposition or (3) as a reward for that condition of the soul which causes one to refrain from retaliation and self-vindication and express oneself in gentleness of behavior

The unsaved look at Christians and decide our blessings must be because of our faithfulness to the church. I believe Isaac's inheritance was by birthright, by obedience AND for his character under pressure—**all three**, and here is why:

Genesis 26:15-16

"15 So the Philistines filled up all of Isaac's wells with dirt. These were the wells that had been dug by the servants of his father, Abraham.

16 Finally, Abimelech ordered Isaac to leave the country. 'Go somewhere else,' he said, 'for you have become too powerful for us.'"

The native Philistines used to drive out foreigners by filling their wells with dirt. So, Isaac with all his wealth was asked to move away from the vicinity of Abimelech's capital in Gerar. He never argued. He just moved some distance to an isolated southern area of the Kingdom of Gerar where his father Abraham had lived. Notice I said he stayed in Gerar. Unlike King Saul, he remained obedient to what God had told him to do. He didn't allow his circumstances to drive him away from **the God-appointed place.** Nowhere does it state that he considered turning back. He recognized that God's timing is not our timing. Isaac's handling of his situation spoke not only to his faith and obedience, but his character under pressure.

He didn't run from his situation and God made room for him, and when his enemies saw that the Lord was with him, they sought peace with him. God will make your enemies your footstool!

Just as Jesus demonstrated in His wilderness experience, it is not our preferences, but our obedience to God's word that enables us to conquer wilderness temptations, and it is the Holy Ghost that keeps His truth before us. If we don't feed on God's word, and we are not filled with His Spirit, it will be impossible to survive these last days.

Saints, we can't afford to lose our souls over this 21st century wilderness. We can't afford to sacrifice our character, our integrity, our values nor our virtue for what is passing away. We have a priceless inheritance with God…one beyond the reach of change and decay. It's not like the job you worked so hard to get that you got laid off of, not like the 401k that lost thousands because of a market crash, not like the one you gave your heart to that disappointed you, or like the home you worked so hard to get that ended up in foreclosure. This is all temporary anyway.

In Strong's Concordance the Greek word for earth is ge', which is defined as a temporary, probationary place to live out our moral preferences in this mortal body. But 2 Corinthians 5:1 (NLT) assures me that when this earthly tent is taken down (that is, when we die and leave this earthly body), we will have a house in heaven, an eternal body made for us by God himself and not by human hands. Chief Apostle Monroe R. Saunders, Sr. said it this way: "Man belongs to eternity, and at eventide, he should return there."

For Jesus said: (John 14:2-3)

"² In my father's house are many mansions: if it were not so, I would have told you. I go to prepare a place for you. ³ And if I go and prepare a place for you, I will come again, and receive you unto myself; that where I am, there ye may be also."

Paul reminds us in Romans 8 that "...the sufferings of this present time are not worthy to be compared with the glory which shall be revealed in us"; and verses 19–23, state that Creation is eagerly waiting for us—for the manifestation of the sons of God; waiting for us to be delivered from corruption. It literally travails with birth pangs. Creation is saying, "Will you humans get yourselves together so that the New Heaven and New Earth can come forth?" Not only that, but those of us who have tasted the first fruits of our eternal redemption are tired of living down here in this mess—knowing we have a home on high.

But we will never find the grace to conquer this 21st-century wilderness and spend eternity with the Lord, as long as we, God's own people, subscribe to the notion that we can accept Jesus as Savior and Lord while refusing to obey His word. It is only through uncompromised OBEDIENCE to the instruction of Almighty God that we will experience life eternal.

References

[1] GotQuestions.Org https://www.gotquestions.org/grace-of-God.html

[2] Phillips, Jenny, "Jesus and Wilderness," American Bible Society Resources

[3] Warnock, George, A Way Through The Wilderness, Chapter 2, The Wilderness of Shur, www.georgewarnock.com/away2.html

[4] Peters-Tanksley, Carol, "The Most Overlook Obstacle to Maturity and Wholeness," drcarol@drcarolministries.com, *July 14, 2022*

[5] Belobaba, George, "Coming Out of Your Wilderness," Breakthrough4Life Ministries, November 22, 2016

[6] Jackson, Mahalia, "Without God I Could Do Nothing" Columbia Records

[7] Erskine, Ralph (1685-1752), Explanatory Notes and Quaint Sayings, On Psalm 27:14, http://www.reformedreader.org/spurgeon/tod/tod27.htm

[8] Scott, Clara H. (1895), "Open My Eyes That I May See"

About the Author

Brenda M. Stokes holds a BA in Psychology from Hampton University where she received a Commission as an Ordnance Officer in the United States Army. She is a graduate of the U.S. Army Command and General Staff College and also holds the degree of Master of Religious Education from Christian Outreach Bible Institute Fayetteville, North Carolina. Upon her retirement from the Army in 1995, Elder Stokes became employed as a Senior Military Analyst and Learning Architect. In 2009, she left corporate America to pursue her greatest passions which include reaching the lost for Christ, ministering to women in all walks of life, and serving as Co-Pastor of United Family Worship Center, Hampton, VA, from which she recently retired. She is an Ordained Elder with the United Church of Jesus Christ (Apostolic). She and her husband, Bishop Lewis

L. Stokes, Sr. are the proud combined parents of nine children (one deceased), twenty-four grandchildren and eleven great-grands.

www.ingramcontent.com/pod-product-compliance
Lightning Source LLC
Chambersburg PA
CBHW071758040426
42446CB00012B/2620